Summary

Operating Forex Trading 4

Chapter 1 - What is Forex Trading 8

   1.1 – How Forex is born 10

   1.2 – The main advantages 19

   1.3 – The subjects in the Forex market........25

   1.4 – Capital management 34

   1.5 – Forex Trading Indices 42

   1.6 – The times at which to trade 47

      1.6.1 – Forex in America 48

      1.6.2 – Forex in Europa 51

      1.6.3 – Forex in Asia 53

   2.1 – Stop-loss...57

   2.2 – Take Profit..62

   2.3 – Market orders 67

2.4 – Limit orders 70

Chapter 3 - Fundamental Analysis and Technical Analysis 74

3.1 – Fundamental Analysis: macroeconomic indicators 80

3.2 – The three pillars of Technical Analysis 85

3.3 – Dow's Theory 89

3.4 – The Momentum and Fibonacci retracements 98

3.5 – Overbought and oversold 103

4.1 – The moving averages 108

4.3 – Relative Strenght Index 112

4.4 – Adverage Directional Index 114

4.5 – The stochastic oscillator 116

Conclusions 119

Operating Forex Trading

The Forex market is the largest financial market in the world, in which currency swaps are made every day for millions of dollars. This is a fair market, not controllable by any institution or government, which changes exclusively in relation to fluctuations in exchange rates. Forex trading consists of buying a currency the moment it sells another, as currency quotes are formed by pairs, such as the Euro-Dollar pair. In the pair, the two currencies take on different roles, one indicates the base currency, while the other represents the quoted currency. The fundamental element that unites them is the exchange price.

The Forex market, as well as that of trading in general, attracts more and more investors. However, there is a great deal of confusion in this, as there is a substantial difference between Forex and stock trading. Forex is a market based on currency trading, while stock trading is based on trading in securities such as stocks or bonds on the stock exchange. Compared to stock trading, Forex has more flexible opening hours, has reduced fees to attract more investors, provides a relatively limited number of currency pairs to facilitate the choice of traders, and does not have any restrictions. Another point in favor of the Forex market is the total absence of intermediaries, with the consequent reduction of platform management costs, which only serve to connect with the market.

The choice between the two investment systems is not simple, especially if you do not have experience in the sector, but to undertake both roads, it is always advisable to carry out a careful study work, with constancy and commitment, because only with sacrifice will it be possible to obtain positive results.

Forex trading is able to guarantee greater stability in relation to the events that can influence the market, so starting to invest its capital in it could prove to be an apt move, but it is fundamental never to lose sight of the limits and the rules of good sense and prudence.

Chapter 1 - What is Forex Trading

The Forex is a market that includes within it all the exchanges of a financial nature that take place between the various subjects, in particular between funding bodies and traders. For this reason, Forex, also known as the currency market, is considered the largest financial market on the entire planet. It derived its name from the union of two words: the first is Foreign which literally means "foreigner", while the second is Exchange So Forex is nothing but a market based on the exchange of foreign currencies. The numbers relating to the

Forex market are truly incredible: every day,the exchange of cash made within it amounts to over 5 trillion US dollars.

One of its main features, which distinguishes it from any other stock market in the world, is its lack of hourly limits, as it is possible to trade at any time throughout the day and night. This aspect should not be underestimated: traders can exploit the consequences generated by international events in real-time, whether they are related to politics, society or the economy.

What also distinguishes the Forex is the total absence of a financial center. This means that the prices relating to the financial instruments traded within it simply react to the market according to the normal law of supply and demand. On the interpretation of this mechanism, traders must act promptly, who will play upwards in the event that the demand for the product observed increases, or downward in the opposite case. The absence of a real headquarters has led Forex to be known worldwide as an "over the counter" market.

1.1 – How Forex is born

The emergence of the Forex market can be traced back to 1944, following the agreements of Bretton Woods, in New Hampshire, between the USA, France and the United Kingdom. This meeting had the purpose of strengthening the individual economies of the participating states, through an international monetary policy, which included the insertion of well-defined procedures and rules. The Forex is the first market in the world, the result of political negotiation, created with the aim of regulating economic relations between the various world nations.

Two projects were presented to reconstruct the monetary and financial system: the first, called White Project, was presented by the American Harry Dexter White, the second, called Keynes Project, was presented by the Englishman John Maynard Keynes. The White Project was focused on the formation of a new body that was supposed to finance all member countries on the basis of the shares of capital subscribed by each of them, in a system based on the US dollar. The Keynes Project foresaw the institution of a new currency, called Bancor, with which the various countries would have had to compensate their debts and credits, based on their economic weight in international trade estimated as the average of the last three years. A compromise emerged between the two projects, but the Piano White gained more weight.

The first fundamental consequence was the establishment of the International Monetary Fund and the World Bank, as institutions with functions of support and supervision over the world economy. In addition, the Bretton Woods agreements for the first time sanctioned the replacement of the British pound with the US dollar as the reference currency for the exchange rate. The value of the dollar was anchored to that of gold: one ounce was priced at $ 35. The states adhering to these agreements had the obligation to control national currency fluctuations with respect to the Dollar, keeping them below a percentage point.

The most significant years for Forex were those between 1950 and 1960. In these years, a large number of operators entered the market and the volume of trade increased considerably.

The monetary system that came into being as a result of the Bretton Woods agreements proved to be efficient since its establishment until the early 1970s. The established rules allowed to achieve the set objectives and to regularize the market, preventing the formation of conflicts. In these years, the United States had to face events that significantly affected national public spendings, such as the war in Vietnam and the expensive Great Society social program. In this situation, public indebtedness coincided with the increase in investors' conversion requests for gold reserves. For this reason, in the summer of 1971, President Nixon decided to suspend this convertibility sanctioned by the previous agreements, announcing this decision at Camp David. Thus at the end of 1971, the G10 finally put an end to the system created following the Bretton Woods agreements. The system dictated by the Smithsonian Agreement, based on flexible exchange rates, began with the necessary devaluation of the US dollar and the consequent fluctuation of exchange rates. The establishment of the new monetary system, with the obvious abatement of the previous one did not lead to the disposal of the institutions founded in 1944, which, outside the GATT, continue to exist today.

The years following the announcement of Camp David are characterized by the leading role of international banks and technology in Forex. In particular, the latter allowed, starting from 1980, to increase trading volumes, thanks to the increase in speed and the expansion of operating hours. The costs and the commissions connected to the trading operations appeared as an obstacle for many insurmountable, and for this reason, until the 90s, the Forex was still considered a market reserved only for a select few, in particular to the banks and to subjects with great financial resources.

The technology, however, has proved once again fundamental for the evolution of Forex, as the advent of the internet has allowed the opening of the trading world also to aspiring traders and investors with limited financial resources. The costs, in fact, have been gradually reduced and trading has increasingly become an open market.

1.2 – The main advantages

The Forex market allows trading on international transactions, with the possibility of obtaining many gains. Many individuals have managed to make Forex trading a real job, but what really distinguishes the Forex from any other market are the advantages connected to the activity carried out.

The main advantage is the low commission costs. Online trading has indeed made it possible to reduce this burden which for years had characterized the financial market. The commissions present today in

Forex are relative to the broker that you choose to use to carry out your business, but they are in any case minimal.

Another advantage regards the full autonomy possessed by the trader. The decision to open a position, to close it, to trade first-hand or to rely on automated systems is entirely up to every investor. In modern trading, the figure of the intermediary is almost completely gone, thanks to the possibility of acting through simple clicks directly on the market. This is possible because Forex has a very high market liquidity, which allows traders to remain active in trading at any time, buying and selling positions in the market.

Another advantageous consequence of the advent of technology in financial markets and in particular in Forex is the possibility to carry out trading at any time of day or night, for five days a week, excluding the weekend during which all financial markets in the world are closed.

Modern trading allows traders to make their own investments, allocating small amounts for each individual transaction. This is possible thanks to the financial leverage tool made available by the brokers, which allows positions to be opened with values significantly higher than the sum invested.

The advent of smartphones and tablets has allowed traders to also expand the concept of trading. The operations can be managed easily from anywhere, with the only requirement being that of having a stable internet connection. In this way, both the chances of exploiting price changes in real-time and, consequently, profits grow. Therefore, it is no longer necessary for the trader to physically go to the bank or, in general, to the financial institution to carry out his transaction.

The sudden increase in the number of aspiring traders, who face the world of Forex often without a sufficient statistical and financial basis, has led brokers to create free demos that allow them to simulate trading activity using a virtual monetary balance, thus eliminating the risks and at the same time allowing them to improve their affinity with the proposed interface.

Finally, trading is often mistakenly seen as an insecure activity. In reality, everything that takes place within the Forex market is constantly monitored and verified by supervisory and control bodies.

Each broker can obtain different certifications, to guarantee the quality of the service offered and the honesty of the activity. This can be translated as total security in the investment that it will make.

1.3 – The subjects in the Forex market

In order to fully understand the Forex, it is essential to know who the subjects are, who in a more or less active way, participate in the movement of prices and in the definition of the meeting point between supply and demand. For many years, the largest financial market in the world has only been opened to a few investors who have certain economic requirements.

Fortunately, the web has marked the definitive opening of Forex to all previously excluded subjects, regardless of the purpose for which they have decided to appear in this market or the way in which they invest. Generally, the subjects decide to carry out trading only for speculative purposes, but a small slice of the active subjects participates in the Forex with the purpose of converting money in currencies different from the one possessed.

The main subjects of Forex are the Merchant Banks, known more simply as business banks. These subjects perform different functions: firstly, being credit institutions, they perform a service related to financial advisory activity and, secondly, they manage assets, sometimes considerable, of private subjects. By not performing commercial functions, it is not possible for private citizens to deposit funds with Merchant Banks. Experts consider these subjects to be the fundamental part of the entire Forex market because, by exploiting their interests, they allow the movement of around 50% of the entire volume of exchanges.

But the Merchant Banks are not the only banking institutions present within Forex. Central Banks are in fact fundamental, which administer national monetary policy, and based on the decisions taken, influence the interest rates present in the Forex market. But the hypothetical power of the central banks is even higher than this. In fact, they periodically make forecasts about future market trends and based on these estimates, traders will make their investments. So this is an indirect but still decisive influence.

There are also institutions that allow traders to bring together the individual capitals in a single investment fund, in order to carry out a single trading activity and to share the profits obtained among the same traders on the basis of the shares assigned. These institutions are called mutual funds.

Instead of the latter, the Hedge Funds, which act within the Forex trying to exploit transactions with a maturity in the very short term, allocating huge investments. Profits are guaranteed, in the case of a positive transaction, thanks to the effect of financial leverage, which is very high in this type of investment. However, in order to access these types of funds, in addition to a high level of economic availability, a series of requirements that limit participation is also required.

The Forex market is also open to multinationals, which exploit the potential of the market to buy certain products or financial instruments in a given currency, to resell them immediately, or at the right time, to another currency. Their purpose is therefore not speculative, but rather that of reducing exchange costs.

Traders represent the last category of subjects that are activated within the Forex market. Of course, whether they are professional investors or not, they act for pure personal profit. Private traders do not enjoy great advantages, which are reserved especially for other subjects. In fact, they cannot get news in advance relating to certain transactions and cannot enjoy reduced spreads.

There are, however, two further categories of subjects that are often heard mentioning within the Forex market, namely bears and bulls. These two animals symbolically represent those who voluntarily influence the market trend. Bulls are those who would like a bull market to make the most of their entry into the Forex with long-term operations. The bears, on the other hand, are more simply the active sellers of Forex, which therefore tend to a bear market to make profits from the trading operations carried out. The market, therefore, fluctuates depending on the strength of these two categories, which continually push the trend up or down. Naturally, a domain of the bulls would translate into a positive trend, with the points of maximum and minimum reaching ever-higher levels, while domination of the bears would lead to a symmetrically opposite situation. For traders, it is convenient that one of the two forces prevails over the other since in case of equilibrium we would find ourselves in one of the lateral phases of the market, during which making profits would prove complex. The names given to active buyers and sellers of Forex are derived from the way in which these two animals attack. The bull tends to enchant the challenger with a movement that goes from the bottom upwards, while the bear tends to attack the preys using the legs, therefore with a movement that goes from top to bottom.

The general opinion that is created by combining the opinions of every single active subject present in the Forex takes the name of market sentiment. Therefore, traders will have to study and investigate what the dominant attitude in the market at that precise moment is, so as to guess what the future trend of the trend may be.

1.4 – Capital management

Trading is an activity in which it is necessary to contemplate risk. This means that opening positions can both bring net profits in the medium-long term, and lead to huge losses affecting the allocated capital. To avoid squandering the entire capital, it is therefore essential to implement a strategy aimed at the management of capital, which is called Money Management. The objective of this analysis is certainly to bring the trader to optimize profits and minimize losses. These cannot be eliminated, as they are inherent in the concept of trading itself, but must be controlled and contained. There are no perfect capital management strategies, and each theory has strengths and weaknesses. However, almost all of them are based on the same key points, to be taken as real Forex dogmas. The lack of a Money Management or in any case the adoption of an unsuitable and little-studied strategy will certainly push the trader to failure.

It is possible to break down the capital management strategy into two components, which can be analyzed separately but which in reality are inseparable from each other. The first component is Risk Management, which consists of analyzing and studying each position that you intend to open in the Forex. The second component is the Position Sizing, which aims to identify what is the optimal amount of capital to be allocated for each transaction to be performed in trading.

Money Management is also risk management. It is necessary to know that the profits necessary to return to the initial capital in case of loss are proportional to the loss.

One of the most important concepts of Money Management and the whole Forex is that of drawdown. This element is nothing more than the reduction of capital due to a series of negative transactions and indicates, in percentage terms, the risk present in the open position. It is essential not to underestimate the drawdown as this establishes what the limit is, based on the allocated capital and the amount of losses, beyond which it becomes impossible to continue trading. An adequate strategy of Money Management tends to define what this limit is, so as to be kept as far as possible from it. As mentioned, although varies, all Money Management strategies are based on some essential aspects. First of all, each trader must have an amount of initial capital that is suitable for trading. Starting in a state of undercapitalization can induce the trader, following an initial series of negative transactions to immediately exit the Forex. At the same time, it is necessary to define what the usable allocated capital limit is. Experts generally advise not to exceed two-thirds of the total capital. Also, for this reason, it is important to intelligently program the operations to be performed. Opening multiple locations at the same time can be beneficial, but also very dangerous. Also, in this case, the advice is to never invest more than 20% of the capital at the same time.

It is important to keep in mind what the objectives of each operation are. The trading must be carried out already determining in advance a maximum limit of loss, which is called stop loss, and a considered optimal level of profit, that is the take profit. Once the trend goes beyond one of the two points, for different reasons, it is recommended to close the position. The reason is to take into consideration a ratio between yield and risk neither too high nor too low. It is sometimes risky and counterproductive to try to let a profit go too far, especially if the take profit point has already been passed. The trend could change orientation and start producing loss, squandering the gain made. For this reason, it is sometimes important to anticipate the closure of a positive transaction in order to make a profit anyway.

A correct application of its capital management strategy will allow traders to remain on the Forex in the long run, even during the negative phases of trading. If the negative operations seem to have no end, the strategy created is not the right one for the Forex and therefore it will be necessary to re-determine the fundamental principles

of Money Management.

1.5 – Forex Trading Indices

The number of trades traded within Forex in a given period represents the volume of market trades. This figure is one of the most important indicators to analyze by traders before entering the Forex market and being decisive in choosing whether or not to open a position.

The volume of trade varies depending on the price trend. Markets with low trading volumes are easily identifiable graphically. They have a substantial equivalence of the level of the prices assumed at the time of opening with the prices of the moment of closure. In addition, the bars or candles that make up the graph are very small. The main feature of the markets with high trading volumes is the considerable distance between maximums and minimums, with very long bars or candles.

Another indicator is called the Percentage in Point, known more simply with the acronym PIP. The Percentage in Point is the change in price suffered by a given currency, however it may be small. Therefore, this instrument is fundamental to verify what the effective variation is, but also allows to establish what the gains and losses are. However, the calculation of the

PIP is very simple. In fact, observing the value assumed by the price at two different times, the PIP corresponds to the difference between the fourth decimal digit of the two values.

As previously stated, the trading market was profoundly different in the past. In fact, in order to invest in Forex, brokers required very high access costs and commissions to possess a sort of selection and control function on the activity carried out by traders. The internet has also allowed other subjects to become Forex brokers and this has led to a natural reduction in market access prices. This was possible thanks to financial leverage, which allowed traders to trade in the Forex lots by taking money in the form of a loan directly from the broker chosen to trade.

The leverage is expressed in the form of a proportion, in which the first number represents the maximum movable value, while the second number is the reference of the invested value. Therefore, in a proportion of 400: 1 for every Euro invested, it is possible to handle a maximum amount of 400 Euro. Of course, the expansion allowed on leverage from financial leverage is also reflected in the losses.

Therefore, both the yield and the risk increase with this tool. For this reason, if trading is done using financial leverage, it becomes fundamental to establish the stop loss and take profit points with great rationality, which will guarantee a balance to the investment.

1.6 – The times at which to trade

One of the characteristics that push traders to invest in the Forex market is the possibility of being able to invest at any time, for five days a week. Specifically, the Forex opens at 11.00 pm on Sunday, taking into consideration the Italian timetable, and closes at the same time on Friday. There are times that allow traders to make more profits and those during which there is both a high volume of trades and a high rate of volatility. Indeed, the combination of these two factors guarantees a much more evident trend, but at the same time, the high volatility induces an increase in the risk rate, caused by the high unpredictability inherent in the movement made by prices. During the opening hours, however, Forex also presents moments in which the volatility and the volume of trade take on values so low that it seems unnecessary to invest or open positions. These are the moments that follow the opening of the market on Sunday, and those that precede Friday closing.

However, it is possible to distinguish three different sessions, which alternate during the day.

1.6.1 – Forex in America

The opening time of the Forex for what concerns the American session is at 14:00 Italian time, while the closing time is 23:00. The American market makes it possible to handle a very high volume of trade. Furthermore, the overlapping and simultaneous trading between the American session and the European session guarantee a favorable situation. During this session, traders must essentially consider two times: the first is 18:00, the second is 20:00, again based on Italian time. In fact, at these times every day, the FED or the US central bank makes announcements that could upset the trends. Therefore the advice is to carry out trading operations only on the US dollar and on the Canadian one once the time of the first announcement made by the Federal Reserve System has been exceeded.

1.6.2 – Forex in Europa

The session in Europe opens at 8:00 am Italian time to close when the FED makes its first announcement, that is, at 6.00 pm. The main feature of this market is the presence of decisive and important movements, which take place mainly starting at 9:00. In fact, starting from this time, news about the variations in the exchange rate of the currencies begin to reach the markets, modifying the trend of the present trends. In this market, the greatest advantages are provided by the transactions carried out on the trading relating to the Euro and those relating to the Swiss Franc.

1.6.3 – Forex in Asia

The Asian session has times that do not coincide with those of the American session and those of the European session. The Forex in Asia opens at the closing time of the American Forex, that is at 23:00 and closes at the opening time of theEuropean Forex, that is at 8:00. It is perhaps the session that moves fewer trade volumes but has large squares that are fundamental for the entire Forex market, such as those in Tokyo and Hong Kong. Having a schedule of activities that is not very influential at a global level from a macroeconomic and financial point of view, the trend seems to take on a linear trend, which does not present excessive fluctuations or real shocks, unless there are really sensational events.

Chapter 2 - Orders in Forex Trading

In the world of online Forex trading, it is possible to make a consistent variety of orders, selecting the instruments with which you want to trade and studying trends in the various markets in real-time through the use of graphical charts. To operate in such markets, it is necessary to have knowledge of the various orders that can be made in the various trading platforms to give the broker precise indications that allow obtaining positive results.

The main types are stop losses, take profits, market orders, and limit orders.

2.1 – Stop-loss

Stop-loss orders are a fundamental tool for traders to manage Forex-related risk, thanks to which it is possible to limit the losses that can arise from a negative phase of the market. For this reason, it is a protection order, through which the maximum value of the loss of capital that the trader is willing to tolerate for a single open position will be set. This order must be set by the trader in advance with respect to the execution of the various opening transactions and will be executed completely automatically by the Forex platform used. When the trend reaches the fixed stop-loss level, the position will be automatically closed to prevent losses from reaching a level that will irreparably erode the capital.

To set the stop-loss point, it is necessary to monitor the volatility of the main currency pairs. If the order is of minor importance, small losses may occur, vice versa, for orders of greater importance, the losses could compromise the totality of the profits of the trader.

Through the stop-loss, it is possible to safeguard the investments from sudden changes in the market, determining the maximum loss achievable based on one's own Forex trading strategy, managing the risk in the most appropriate way.

The greatest losses occur when the trade is closed and the stop-loss order is executed at a time when the market is going through a phase of changes that could generate profits instead. In this case, it is possible to set the strategy in such a way that additional positions are opened to recover the losses previously incurred. However, even this system can prove to be a failure, as the market often suffers from sudden changes, due to the diffusion of important financial news, which is unable to make profits, but leads to further losses.

The stop-loss order is the basis for building an efficient trading strategy. For this reason, three systems of stop values will be generated based on the volatility of the trade: a system with a high stop for cases of high volatility, a system with a low stop for cases of low volatility, an intermediate system. Automatic trading systems analyze the signals to assess the level at which to set the stop-loss.

Traders do not always adhere to established stop-loss orders but continue to keep positions at a loss in the hope that the trend will change its trend and turn losses into profits. However, this interference with the implemented strategy will only generate larger losses, putting the entire capital at risk.

2.2 – Take Profit

The second type of fundamental orders for the management of Forex trading operations is take profit. It stands in contrast to the stop-loss and indicates the level of protection of profits. Like the stop-loss, it must be set before executing market transactions, based on the trader's strategy and financial availability. In a sense, it is a limit to earnings, which is activated once the previously established levels are reached, to prevent market changes from eroding these gains and nullifying what has been done up to that point.

What takes the take profit is a purely prudential function. At the same time, a trader can doubt that the trade, once it has gone beyond the take profit level, can continue in its positive trend and the closure of the early position could prove to be a missed opportunity. But the task of take profit can also be understood as a limit to the trader's greed, which could lead to higher earnings, but also very large losses. Human emotion is a characteristic that in the world of Forex should be completely zeroed. Greed naturally falls within the feelings to be eliminated, and letting go of profit means facing a risk that becomes higher every second. However, choosing the exact point in which to place the take profit is not easy. The choice may depend essentially on the motivation that pushes the trader to make a certain investment, which can be mainly attributed to two cases: the first involves the identification of a specific graphic figure that the trend is going to complete; the second relates to the pursuit of the trend undertaken by the trend. If the trader has identified a partial figure by analyzing the graph of the price fluctuation, investing on the conclusion of the trend, the take profit must be fixed at the point where it is assumed that the representation that led to the opening of the position will be concluded. The decision of where to fix the take profit in the event that the trader opens the position in order to follow a specific trend is instead subordinated to the levels of support and resistance. These represent fundamental points since it is assumed that in the areas in which the same are present, the trend can reverse its trend. Of course, in the event that the investment refers to a purchase transaction, the take profit must be positioned below the resistance level; vice versa, in a sales transaction, the take profit will have to be set a few points above the support level.

2.3 – Market orders

Market orders must be conceived as communications that each trader sends to their broker: the communication involves the willingness to buy at the selling price present at a given time or to sell at the demand price present at the time the transaction is opened.

For simplification, in market orders, the offer price is indicated with the abbreviation ASK, while the demand price with the abbreviation BID; the difference between the two price values is known as SPREAD.

The market order does not require any requirement to be executed, except the will of the trader, and its opening is immediate. However, it is possible to distinguish two different types of market orders, first type is called long orders, and the second type is called short orders.

The first type refers to purchase orders that the trader decides to execute when he or she is convinced that the price of the instrument observed may experience a rise in subsequent periods.

The second type represents a category of orders attributable to short selling. These types of orders are executed by the trader when he or she assumes that the trend can move downwards in a very short term.

2.4 – Limit orders

If the market orders do not require any particular requirement for their execution, the limit orders require the occurrence of a specific event in order to be executed. The trading platform used will place the investment immediately, but the same will be executed only if the price trend exceeds the limit that the trader has previously set. It is possible to execute four different types of limit orders.

The first type is called Buy Limit, and it is an order that is used if the trader expects the price trend to continue the downward trend. However, the operation will be performed by opening a buying position when the trend exceeds a certain limit, thus anticipating the trend reversal. To carry out an order of this kind, the condition must be set at a lower price than the one present at the time of the investment.

A second category is the Buy Stop order. The trader, in this case, expects a continuation of the price trend but will open a long position only after the trend has reached a certain limit. In this case, the level of the limit must be set at a higher point than the value possessed by the price at the time the position is opened.

Sell Limit orders, on the other hand, are used if the trader intends to open a short position, but before opening the position, he or she wants to make sure that the downward trend reaches a certain level. Also, in this case, the requirement that determines the effective realization of the trading is the achievement of a condition set at a lower value than the one possessed by the price at the time of the order.

Finally, the last type of orders is represented by Sell Stop orders. The trader expects the price to continue its upward trend but once a certain limit is reached, it reverses its performance. Therefore the point at which the Sell Stop is set must be at a higher level than the price at the time the order is placed.

Chapter 3 - Fundamental Analysis and Technical Analysis

In the world of Forex, the study of all the macroeconomic events that are able to manipulate, or at least influence the price trend and the entire market trend is very important. This type of analysis is called macroeconomic analysis, but it is known to all traders as Fundamental Analysis. The purpose of the Fundamental Analysis is to identify the economic news related to a specific country and try to understand how the announcements of such news affect the value of the currency traded in that country. However, the Fundamental Analysis refers to an economic calendar, containing all the events, identified both according to a chronological criterion and according to a national criterion, which could influence the level of the various currencies. The web now abounds with economic calendars, more or less detailed, and for traders it is easier to identify and wait for economic news. The most complete economic calendars make it possible to relate the data relating to an economic event with those present on the same day in previous years, but also with those expected for the current year, so as to provide traders with a clear and complete overview based on which it is possible to carry out an in-depth study of Fundamental Analysis. The tools needed to carry out a correct fundamental analysis are the macroeconomic indicators. Being aware of the presence or otherwise of certain economic news is the first step that every trader, professional or not, must take before trading.

If Fundamental Analysis studies the economic news and their impact on the world of Forex, the Technical Analysis, through a detailed analysis relating to the trend of prices within the market, aims to define what their behavior could be in a more or less distant future. To do this, the Technical Analysis relies on various statistical tools, but also tends to evaluate the human behaviors that, according to this theory, influence trend oscillations more than anything else. The Technical Analysis has its primary purpose of identifying and analyzing all the possible levels of entry and exit from the market in such a way that the trader can choose the best entry, thanks to certain tools increasingly advanced from the technological point of view. There are essentially two instruments on which the

Technical Analysis is based: first of all the technical indicators, which on the basis of the statistical data in possession, provide interesting information regarding the price trend; secondly, the graphic tools, which work more on the visual part to offer the trader a clear image of the market trend. Of course, both tools require analysis software capable of transposing data and externalizing it in the best possible way so that it can be understood by the trader. These softwares are readily available on the web: sometimes, however, the work done is not sufficiently clear and detailed, in particular if it is a matter of software downloaded for free from the Internet.

3.1 – Fundamental Analysis: macroeconomic indicators

As previously stated, Fundamental Analysis bases its effectiveness on some macroeconomic indicators.

The first of these indicators is certainly the national Gross Domestic Product, also known with the acronym PIL. This indicator is given by the sum of all the goods and services that are produced within the national boundaries in a given period of time, to then be consumed. The Gross Domestic Product greatly influences the Forex, as a possible announcement of its increase involves a positive phase, vice versa its reduction is closely related to a market contraction.

A second macroeconomic indicator which is very important for Fundamental Analysis is the data relating to industrial production. This figure, not considering the building sector, indicates what production refers to the industrial sector of a given country only. Also in this case, as for GDP, industrial production and Forex are proportional and the increase in the former determines an expansive phase of the latter, while a decline would cause a negative phase.

Fundamental Analysis can also rely on an indicator that aims to exclude all indirect sales, including services, from GDP and is called a retail sales index. Also for this macroeconomic indicator, the relationship with Forex is strictly proportional.

The indicator relating to durable goods orders refers to the volume expressed in the national currency of durable goods, that is, those goods that offer their utility over several years, such as cars, which have been produced by the manufacturing sector of a nation. The market strengthens when this indicator increases and weakens when the indicator decreases.

Interest rates are also among the indispensable macroeconomic indicators for Fundamental Analysis, as they affect both the monetary policy implemented by central banks and the economic choices of a country. In this case, the effects caused by an increase in interest rates are double: initially an increase is obtained in the volatility rate present in the Forex. Subsequently, this translates into an expansion of the market. Conversely, a reduction in the rate causes a weakening of the market.

Through the relationship between the incidence of the employed population and the total population of a given country, it is possible to know the national employment indicator. Positive values of this indicator determine favorable market phases, on the contrary, negative values lead to phases of decline.

The difference between exports and imports, that is the national trade balance, determines the last of the main macroeconomic indicators that influence the Forex market.

3.2 – The three pillars of Technical Analysis

As mentioned above, the Technical Analysis is aimed at forecasting the trend of financial markets, to allow those who intend to carry out investment transactions to be able to make profits with greater probability. This analysis is very complex and is based on three basic assumptions: prices discount everything, the market moves by trends and history repeats itself.

The first assumption indicates that the prices on the market reflect all the economic information available, even those known only to a few subjects. Therefore, it is not necessary to research and analyze this information, as it is already contained in price fluctuations.

The second assumption indicates that price fluctuations are never random, but the result of the combination of two or more trends. The Technical Analysis aims to identify these trends and predict their evolution over time. Therefore the trader in the context of this analysis will not have to pretend to sell at the maximum price levels or to buy at the minimum levels but will have to exploit the trend in place at that time.

The third prerequisite indicates the cyclical nature of the financial market trend. This aspect is mainly due to the willingness of human beings to make profits from trading, which leads them to periodically repeat the same behaviors, sometimes even in a frenetic way. It is therefore important to analyze the time series, which tend to identify price patterns useful for understanding what the trend of the trend may be in the future.

The assumptions of the Technical Analysis do not guarantee the infallibility of the forecasts but aim to formulate forecasts with a percentage of correctness equal to at least 70%, to be able to extricate even the most hostile financial markets.

3.3 – Dow's Theory

The Modern Technical Analysis is the result of a series of studies carried out by an American, Charles Dow, a journalist who in the early twentieth century published a series of theories concerning the analysis of financial markets in the Wall Street Journal. These theories have been used as a basis for the study and examination of further doctrines, because of the effectiveness and adaptability shown also for the systems present in modern markets.

Dow's theory is based on the idea that price fluctuations do not depend on purely random factors, but that these depend on certain trends, more or less predictable. These oscillations are also compared by the journalist to the waves of the sea, which periodically advance and retract, depending on the tides. Only when the trends come to almost completely exhaust their strength, then will there be a reversal of the trend and the cyclicality will resume from the beginning.

Dow, in order to organize his theory, set six fundamental points of his analysis.

The first assumption of Dow's theory also coincides with one of the basic principles of

Technical Analysis, namely that according to which prices discount everything. So according to Dow, the price contains in itself all the information, even those that are difficult to find, and it is sufficient to analyze it to become aware of the economic events that have characterized it.

The second point of Dow's Theory identifies three different possible trends that can be assumed by the price within the financial market, which differ only in duration. The first type is called as the primary trend, which has a significantly longer duration than the other two categories, as it can follow its trend fluctuation even for periods longer than one year. The second type is called the secondary trend, which has a variable duration between ninety and one hundred and eighty days. Finally, the last type is called the minor trend, which generally lasts less than a month and is not always easily identifiable on the market.

In the third point, Dow proceeds in his theory by breaking down every single type of trend into three further categories, which are called phases, so as to facilitate understanding of the market and identifying the motivations that drive prices towards recruitment of a certain trend. The first of the three phases is defined by Dow as an

Accumulation phase, and it is fundamental because during this interval, the trend begins to take shape. However, only a few traders will be able to get to know the economic information and fully exploit this awareness. The trend is still in one of its lateral phases and shows no intention of varying its oscillation. Therefore, it is impossible to graphically recognize that it is in an accumulation phase. The second phase, known as the Participation phase, shows the first signs that can be distinguished also graphically from the formation of a new trend, as we are witnessing an initial price increase. The increasingly consistent entry into the market of traders, even those not informed, pushes the price level ever higher until this influence diminishes causing the trend to slow. It is certainly the phase of the trend most favorable for investors, during which the market presents very high trading volumes and a level of volatility. The third phase, finally, is defined by Dow as a Distribution phase and represents the time interval during which the price has reached its maximum and investors intuit that it is the opportune moment to close the open positions in the Forex, decreeing the trend reversal. It is a very hectic phase because the traders have entered a state similar to panic, to be able to sell the position at the best possible price, and start a frantic race to the bottom.

Analyzing the rail and US industrial index, Dow was able to identify a direct correlation between the two, an event that allowed him to establish the fourth point of his theory. According to Dow, these two indexes have an indissoluble positive link that makes it unable to confirm a trend reversal if this situation is observed only in one of the two. This concept can also be applied to the currencies of various countries in the Forex market.

The fifth point envisages another method of identifying the trend, which is derived, according to Dow, from the observation of the trading volumes present within the market. They are sometimes even able to anticipate the trend, but they must be analyzed above all in order to confirm it. In fact, each trend is associated with a significant increase in volumes, while the lateral phases present substantial reductions in them. This means that it is possible to confirm that there is a trend only after verifying the expansion of the volumes..

The sixth point in Dow's Theory is perhaps the most complicated. He states that every trend must be considered as such until a clear sign of the inversion appears in the graph. Until then, especially for those who adopt a Trend Following strategy, it is necessary to follow the trend. Clearly, it is complicated to anticipate the reversal of the trend, especially when there is a price drop due to a financial correction.

3.4 – The Momentum and Fibonacci retracements

Once the trend has been identified, each investor, in order to increase the probability of success, must analyze both the structure and the intensity. In particular this last feature, known in the Forex also as Momentum, gives the opportunity to understand if the trend can last a long time or if it is running out of its strength, turning towards a lateral market phase. Furthermore, finding out which is the Momentum offers traders the chance to guess, through the analysis called market divergences, when the end of the trend will occur.

The concept of Momentum has deep ties with physics and in particular with Newton's three laws. It is necessary to imagine that prices are like bodies, while the subjects that influence Forex are forces: both components respond to the laws of dynamics composed by the English mathematician.

Following this logic, the prices and the active subjects of the market can become the protagonists of the three laws of dynamics. According to the first law, prices are subject to fluctuations according to the announced economic news, and always on the basis of it, the subjects will enter the market. For the second law, the thrust and intensity of the trend will be proportional to the number of subjects who decide to purchase the positions. Finally, according to the third law, once the maximum point is reached, the price trend will undergo a push of equal magnitude, completely opposite, which will lead to a trend reversal.

The correlation between physics and financial markets helps to understand what the importance of momentum is. It, in fact, intended as a variation of the intensity of the trend in a given time interval, undergoes increases when the price trend is subject to important accelerations: a high momentum indicates that the trend will continue in the trend direction.

The momentum assumes high values only on three occasions: firstly, when the trend is forming, or when there is a trend reversal and finally during the lateral market phases. Studying the momentum allows us to guess what the future price trend may be, helping the trader to accumulate profits.

Currently, it is possible to identify the momentum through the use of some indicators, among which we recall the moving averages, the Bollinger bands, the RSI, the ADX and the stochastic oscillator.

In order to identify the possible levels that the price can take in the immediate future, many traders decide to use the Fibonacci retracements. The latter was an Italian mathematician who lived in 1200, who had identified a sort of proportion between any two elements, even those found in nature, which have different sizes. Fibonacci, based on a hypothetical golden section, identifies a sequence of numbers, in which each digit is given by the sum of the last two numbers preceding it. This sequence has been successfully applied also in the world of trading and is now a very important tool that traders use to analyze the market.

The purpose of Fibonacci retracements is to identify some points, which no other instrument is able to detect, which could become supports or resistances. In this way, the trader is able to anticipate a trend reversal, obtaining considerable advantages.

3.5 – Overbought and oversold

In Forex there are situations in which prices reach certain levels, located in particular areas of the market.

In particular, the overbought zone refers to an area in which the price trend is found which has suffered an excessive rise. So once the trend has reached this area, the traders expect that there will be a reversal of the trend that brings prices back into a standard range. The prices reach these areas on extraordinary occasions and remain there for a relatively short time. The excessive rise is caused by the struggle between bulls and bears that characterizes the financial market. Initially, the excessive rise caused the bulls, that is the buyers, to close the open positions on the market in order to make profits. At the same time, bears, or sellers, have taken advantage of the situation by selling in the open. All this is reflected graphically with an initial surge of the trend towards the overbought area and a subsequent dive for a return to normality.

Symmetrically, the oversold areas identify those downgraded areas where prices have gone, exceeding the minimum periodic limits. In this case, the traders expect a surge that brings the trend back to the standard average of the period. Even the reasons are opposite to those that create surges in the overbought areas. In this case, the bears, due to the excessively low price, decided to close their positions, while the bulls hypothesized that the trend could soon be traced, opening positions. These actions first sank the trend beyond the periodic minimum, and then returned it to its standard range.

Chapter 4 - Indicators and oscillators

In order to analyze Forex more thoroughly, a series of indicators or oscillators have been made available to traders. These are intended to confirm or deny the credibility of each individual signal received. There is nothing certain in the world of trading. Therefore, it is wrong to think that indicators and oscillators can somehow predict the future, indicating with certainty the values that the prices will assume. They must be thought of as support tools, which increase the chances of earning, but which are certainly not infallible.

4.1 – The moving averages

Moving averages are the most used indicator by investors in Forex and other financial markets. Thanks to this type of indicator, it is possible to outline the tendency that the market will take on, but also to generate some signals so that the trader can promptly open or close a certain position. Moving averages can be divided into three sub-categories: the simple moving average, the weighted one and the exponential one. These differ from each other depending on the calculation method, giving greater weight to the events of the past that are more distant, as is the case for the exponential moving average, or more recent, as is the case for the weighted moving average.

The use of moving averages makes it possible to identify the primary trend, reducing all those corrections that distort the attention of the trader and which cause valuation errors during the trading activity.

4.2 - Bollinger bands

Through the Bollinger bands the trader can identify the volatility present in the market and report it directly on the chart. This indicator is composed of three lines: the upper band, the lower band, and the balance line. The first band moves above the price line, the second below it, while the third follows the moving average of price values. This indicator has many functions. First of all, it is used to identify the volatility present in the market: the bands widen when the volatility is high and shrink when the volatility takes on low values. Furthermore, the Bollinger bands are used to confirm the intensity of a given trend and to identify the overbought and oversold areas. Finally, this oscillator makes it possible to determine the areas in which supports and resistances are present.

This tool can be very useful especially if used in combination with other indicators, to evaluate, and eventually confirm, the meaning of market signals.

4.3 – Relative Strenght Index

The Relative Strength Index, better known with the acronym RSI, is an indicator of fundamental importance for the execution of trading as it helps to evaluate the correct speed with which prices change. It is one of the most used indicators that, although difficult to understand, is inserted by the brokers directly into the platforms so that traders can use it without difficulty.

The RSI makes it possible to understand the area to which the price belongs at a particular moment and, in particular, identifies the overbought and oversold areas, thus allowing investors to open the positions correctly.

Generally, the range in which the Relative Strength Index moves is between the value 0 and the value 100. This allows us to always have objective data, regardless of the observed trend. This indicator takes specific values to indicate that the trend is in particular areas and specifically: the RSI is above 70 if the price is in an overbought zone, and is less than 30 if the price is found in an oversold area.

4.4 – Adverage Directional Index

Through the Adverage Directional Index, it is possible to understand what the actual strength or intensity of a trend is. This indicator, also known by the acronym ADX, is graphically represented by a line that oscillates between 0 and 100: the trend appears strong if the ADX takes values greater than 40, while it is considered congested when it takes values below 20.

Therefore, using this indicator, it is not possible to understand if the trend is in a rising or falling phase, but only if one is or is not in a trend phase.

The ADX consists of three lines: the Line + DI, calculated on the basis of the difference between the maximum of the current day and that of the previous day; the Line −DI, calculated on the basis of the difference between the minimum of the current day and that of the previous day; the ADX Line, which is based on the relationship between the two previous lines.

Based on the values assumed by these three lines, the trader can guess whether the market is in a trend phase or not.

4.5 – The stochastic oscillator

If the trader intends to identify which time intervals are characterized by accumulation or by price distribution, then it is necessary to use the stochastic oscillator. This is one of the most powerful tools of the entire market analysis, able to understand what the probable future price trend is. The stochastic oscillator examines the position taken by the closing prices: if these are approaching the maximum daily levels, then the trend will probably be on the upside, while if they approach the daily minimums the trend will tend to fall. Also, in this case, the range assumes values that oscillate between the value 0 and the value 100.

The analysis of the stochastic oscillator is based on two elements. First of all, the Curve% K, which relates the closing prices in a given interval, and secondly the Curve% D, which instead operates on the levels assumed by the first curve. In this case, the overbought areas are identified when the oscillator takes values greater than 80, while those of oversold are assumed to have values below 20.

In short, with the stochastic user, it is possible to identify, in addition to the overbought and oversold areas, also the areas that anticipate trend reversals. It also sends the trader signals for opening or closing the position, based on the data obtained by crossing the% K and% D curves.

Conclusions

The analysis carried out in this guide has shown that Forex can be a winning bet, especially if done in a professional manner.

Of course, the risk of suffering losses cannot be eliminated completely, but by implementing an efficient strategy, through the study and analysis of the various indicators, it will be possible to reduce the incidence and protect the capital invested.

Being aware of the risk is the first fundamental step to increase the chances of achieving positive results in the Forex market. Thanks to this sort of limit it will be possible to avoid suffering serious losses and at the same time obtaining reasonable profits.

www.ingramcontent.com/pod-product-compliance
Lightning Source LLC
Chambersburg PA
CBHW060853220526
45466CB00003B/1349